A POCKET GUIDE

TO ANGLESEY COASTAL FLOWERING PLANTS

Published by Gareth Rowlands

Copyright Gareth Rowlands

All rights reserved

ISBN 978-1-5272-3791-9

March 2019

Design and layout: jenksdesign@yahoo.co.uk
Printed by Cambrian Printers, Aberystwyth, Wales

Sunset at South Stack (right)
©Andy Rowlands
andyrowlands.com

A POCKET GUIDE

TO ANGLESEY COASTAL FLOWERING PLANTS

GARETH ROWLANDS

INTRODUCTION

THIS POCKET GUIDE will help you explore the beautiful coastline of Anglesey - the island's wildflowers found in a variety of habitats, from cliffs and heathland, sand dunes and shingle beaches to mud flats and salt marshes.

The guide is organised according to plant families with the characteristics of selected families described. Successful flowering plant identification is no easy task and only comes with practise and experience. It is an advantage to recognise some of the major plant families such as the carrot family, the cabbage family and orchid family. A starting point is to compare the plant to the photographs in the guide. The next step is to consider the description of the plant including characteristics such as leaf arrangement and flower anatomy. Although many plants are able to live in a variety of habitats, many of those found around the coast have adapted special features enabling them to grow and survive extreme conditions. It follows that sand dunes, for example, will generally have a definite number of species, making identification a less daunting task.

- The location guide indicates the habitat where the plant may be found.
- Where appropriate included in the descriptions are culinary uses
- Medicinal uses of the plant
- Other interesting information

References to culinary or medicinal uses of selected species of plants are for interest only and should not be considered as a recommendation for their use. Many medicinal applications can be beneficial but a medical expert should always be consulted before making any changes or additions to prescribed medications. Herbs should be used carefully in moderation as concentrated doses of some species can be extremely harmful. Herbs, like medications, are potent and must be taken wisely and with caution because they may interact with other medications. Herbs rarely cure diseases but they may help to relieve symptoms.

COASTAL HABITATS

The coast is a challenging habitat for plants. Their survival depends on being able to overcome the hazards of strong wind, high salinity and thin soil in a continuously changing environment. In order to flourish, many flowering plants have become adapted to grow on different types of shore. To aid identification they are grouped as cliffs and heathland, sand dunes, shingle beach, and mudflats and salt marshes.

CLIFFS AND HEATHLAND

The vegetation is dominated by a few species of which Heather and Gorse are most common. High winds and thin, acid soils mean that transpiration rate is high. Many of the plants are xerophytes.

SAND DUNES

Conditions here are extreme with rapid drainage, little or no humus, high wind speed and salt spray from the sea. The establishment of Marram Grass helps to shelter, stabilise and add humus to the soil enabling other less hardy plants to colonise the dunes.

SHINGLE BEACH

Shingle is a particularly unstable habitat as stones are moved about by the action of the waves. Many of the plants are adapted to withstand high salinity. Sea Beet and Sea Kale are commonly found.

MUDFLATS AND SALT MARSHES

The soil is frequently submerged by the tides and contains decomposing plant materials, consequently oxygen levels are low. Halophytes such as Sea Aster and Rock Samphire are adapted to live in these conditions.

FLOWERING PLANT IDENTIFICATION

To identify Angiosperms or Flowering Plants some knowledge of plant structure is required. The flower is the reproductive part of the plant. Many species have flowers that are hermaphrodite, that is, the individual flowers contain both male and female organs. A unisexual flower possesses either stamens or carpels but not both. When separate male and female flowers are found on a single individual plant it is called monoecious but when male flowers are on one plant and female flowers are on another plant this is termed dioecious. Flowers of different species exhibit a great variety in their appearance but similar patterns can be observed.

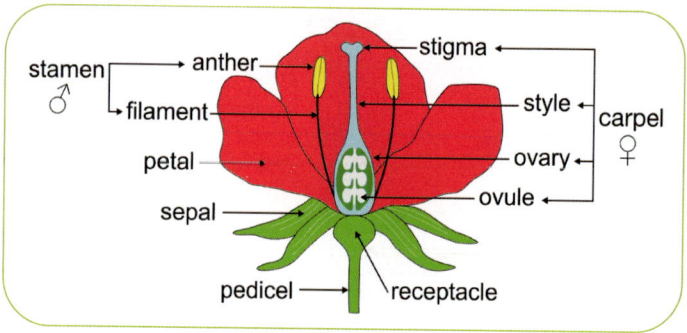

A typical insect-pollinated flower consists of four main components or whorls arranged from the outside to the centre.

* Sepals - the outer whorl or calyx, usually green and protect the flower in bud.
* Petals - the next whorl or corolla and consists of the petals.
* The two innermost whorls are the stamens and the carpels, containing the male and female reproductive organs of the flower respectively. These may be enclosed within the petals or protrude from the flower.

  * Stamen - the male organ, each consisting of a long, slender stalk or filament at the end of which are the pollen sacs or anthers containing pollen.
  * Carpel - the female part, made up of the ovary which contains the eggs or ovules. Projecting from the ovary is the stalk-like style which ends in the stigma.

CENTAURIUM LITTORALE (SEASIDE CENTAURY)

- A flower may be simple, where the petals are separate, or more complex where the petals are fused to form a tube. A flower may be regular in shape (actinomorphic) and can be divided into two equal parts in any plane (radially symmetrical).

EPIPACTIS PALUSTRIS (MARSH HELLEBORINE)

- A flower may be irregular in shape (zygomorphic) and can be divided only by a single plane into two equal parts (bi-laterally symmetrical).

LEAF SHAPE AND ARRANGEMENT ARE A USEFUL AID IN IDENTIFICATION

Leaves have two overall types of shape:

- Simple leaves, with or without teeth around the margins, are individually attached to the stem with one blade and have an independent vein structure.
- Compound leaves consist of many smaller leaflets that attach to the main leaf stem.

There are 3 types of leaf arrangement:

- Opposite - two leaves arise from the stem at the same level (at the same node) and are positioned opposite to each other.
- Alternate - the leaves are single at each node and are situated along the stem alternately in an ascending spiral.
- Whorled – when there are three or more equally spaced leaves at a node.

FLOWERING PLANT FAMILIES

A family is a group of genera (sing. genus) that are all more closely related to each other than they are to other genera i.e. they share similar characteristics. Botanists recognise 416 flowering plant families. All plant families have Latin names that end with the suffix – aceae or ae. For example, *Apiaceae* and *Brassicaceae*.

Key features common to flowering plant families include the following:
- Flower shapes -the petals can be separate or fused to form a tube. The simplest flowers are regular but some plants such as orchids have more complex, irregular flowers.
- Flower arrangement - the flowers may be solitary or single, each one growing on a separate stalk or they may be grouped in clusters.
- Number of petals and sepals - the simplest flowers tend to have 5 petals.
- Number of stigmas or stamens.
- Leaf shape - single or divided into leaflets.
- Leaf arrangement - alternate leaves may grow singly along the stem; opposite leaves are arranged in pairs; whorled leaves are arranged in rings.
- Fruits - these may be soft and juicy, others hard and dry such as pods and capsules.

Many plants grow in particular habitats, which helps in identifying flowers

The ability to recognise species of wild flowers only comes with experience. It therefore helps to learn to recognise the major families. Beginners will spend a considerable amount of time trying to match a plant specimen to the photographs in the book. The fact that plants will be expected to be found in certain habitats should ease the task of identification. Some plants seem to be able to grow in a wide range of habitats but others only grow under a particular set of conditions. This book describes plants living around the coast of Anglesey, where many have adapted to overcome harsh habitats. For example, plants growing on the cliffs of South Stack and the surrounding heathland are subjected to dry, well drained, acid soils, with exposure to direct sunlight and high winds. Salt marsh plants or halophytes grow in deep mud which is frequently submerged by the tide.

IDENTIFYING PLANT FAMILIES

The three largest flowering plant families containing the greatest number of species are the Daisy family (Asteraceae) with about 24,000 species, the Orchid family (Orchidaceae) with about 20,000 species, and the Pea family (Fabaceae) with 18,000 species.

For selected flowering plant families the main features are described followed by examples of species of flowering plants found in the coastal habitats of Anglesey.

Family Amaranthaceae: Goosefoots, Oraches
Difficult to identify. Drab plants that favour the strandline.
Small flowers may be hermaphrodite in Goosefoots; unisexual in Oraches.
In the latter, male flowers have 5 green sepals, no petals; female flowers lack both petals and sepals.
Stems, roots, leaves of many species are red in colour.
Simple leaves sometimes succulent or hairy, usually arranged alternately along the stems.
Fruit may be a capsule, utricle, nutlet, drupe or berry.

Glassworts are a group of highly specialised halophytes. They appear to be merely jointed, succulent stems lacking leaves but on closer examination can be observed to possess reduced, minute scale-like triangular leaves. The inconspicuous flowers are pollinated by wind. Annual. Height 10-45cm.
❀ Aug-Sep.

🔴 Middle and upper zones of salt marshes.

🍴 In Britain it is one of several plants known as 'samphires' and are often served as an accompaniment to fish. After cooking, the edible flesh is removed from the hard stringy core and covered in butter or olive oil. Its bright green stalks resemble asparagus spears, hence one of its alternative names – Sea Asparagus. Once described as the poor man's Asparagus it is now much in demand as a culinary speciality. A high quality edible oil, similar to safflower oil, is obtained from the seeds.

🟡 Glassworts include halophyte plants from several genera. In Britain there are 7 species of Glassworts as well as numerous hybrids. The photograph shows the bulbous segments typical of *S.europeae agg.* of which *S.ramosissima* is a member. The plants shown are green but their foliage turns red in autumn. The ashes of burnt Glasswort plants were once an important ingredient in making glass and soap.

Family Amaranthaceae   Annual Sea-blite
(Suaeda maritima)   Helys Unflwydd

The fleshy, succulent leaves are short, roundish, flat on the upper surface and taper to a blunt tip. The tiny green flowers (sometimes purple or red) lack petals; 5 succulent green sepals. Found in small bunches in the axils of leaves. Annual. Height to 30cm.

Jul-Sep.

Abundant on salt marshes.

The young leaves and seeds may be eaten raw or cooked and have a pleasant, salty flavour making a tasty addition when added in small quantities to a salad. The young shoots are pickled in vinegar and eaten on their own or used as a relish.

The leaves absorb a great deal of salt and eventually turn red when oversaturated. If the salt is extracted from the leaves and left to dry it turns black and the resultant ashes provide a soda that is used in making glass and soap.

Family Amaranthaceae Frosted Orache
(Atriplex laciniata) Llygwyn Arianaidd

🌺 Found in sprawling patches, the silvery-white, diamond-shaped leaves are borne on well branched reddish stems. The small yellow-green flowers are in clusters in the leaf axils. Annual. Height 6-30cm. 🌼 Jul-Oct.

📍 Strandline of sandy and shingle beaches.

Family Amaranthaceae Sea Beet
(Beta vulgaris subsp. maritima) Betysen Arfor

Upright stems bear large lower leaves with upper leaves becoming smaller, narrower and lacking stalks. The leafy spikes bear tiny, green flowers in clusters. Perennial. Height to 1m. ❀ Jun-Sep.

Frequent around the coast. Margins of salt marshes.

The whole plant is edible; the spikes of green flowers, the reddish stems and the beetroot-like roots. The young root is sweet and tender and can be grated in salads. The roots can be cooked and used as a vegetable; they are sweet and delicious when baked. Leaves may be eaten raw or cooked like spinach. The saltiness makes it a great addition to a fish dish.

In ancient times the leaves and roots of Sea Beet were used in the treatment of several diseases, particularly tumours. Sea Beet juice has also been used to treat ulcers.

Family Amaranthaceae   Prickly Saltwort

(Salsola kali subsp. kali) Helys Ysbigog

A highly-branched, dark-green and rather sprawling plant with fleshy, short, linear and succulent leaves tipped by sharp spines. Very small flowers. Annual. Height 20–60cm.
☀ Jul-Sep. Vulnerable.

Sandy shores just above the strandline.

🍴 An excellent food with a crunchy tender texture. Young leaves and stems may be eaten raw or cooked and can be used as a spinach substitute or added in small quantities to salads.

📋 The juice of the fresh plant is an excellent diuretic. Salsolin, one of the constituents of the plant, has been used to regulate blood pressure.

✋ Ashes of the burnt plant were at one time used for making glass and soap. Large quantities of the ashes were imported into Britain for this purpose but nowadays a chemical process using salt is employed. The ashes can also be used as a cleaner for fabrics.

Family Apiaceae: Umbellifers - Parsley or Carrot family

Fairly easy to recognise because most have umbrella-shaped flower heads.

Flowers, small with 5 petals, most are white.

Flowers in terminal umbels (a flat-topped or domed cluster of flowers).

Stems are usually, but not always, hollow.

Most are aromatic herbs with alternate, feather-divided leaves that are encased at the base.

Family Apiaceae Wild Carrot

(Daucus carota subsp. carota) Moronen y Maes

Solid ridged stems with leaves divided into leaflets. The white compound umbel (with central flower sometimes purple) rests on top of a distinctive green collar of long, leafy, downward pointing bracts. Biennial. Height to 100cm. ❀ Jun-Aug.

Common on sandy soils near the sea. Also in patches on exposed sea cliffs.

The oil is used to flavour alcoholic and non-alcoholic beverages, as well as a variety of food products. The seeds are aromatic.

Wild Carrot is used for urinary tract ailments including kidney stones, bladder problems, water retention and also to treat gout.

Wild Carrot seed oil is used to fragrance toiletries and detergents.

Family Apiaceae Sea Carrot
(Daucus carota subsp. gummifer)   Moronen y Môr

Splayed flowering stems bearing white, occasionally pinkish, flowers. Small flowers at the centre with larger, more irregular flowers at the periphery. Large finely divided bracts below the flower heads. Leaves divided into many deeply-lobed leaflets. In Sea Carrot the umbels, when in fruit, are flat or convex, unlike the umbels of Wild Carrot which are concave. Also the hairless leaves are darker and more fleshy than those of Wild Carrot.
Biennial. Height to 100cm. ✿ Jun–Aug. Nationally scarce.

On sandy soils near the sea.

Recent evidence suggests that when prepared as an essential oil the plant has antifungal and anti-inflammatory properties.

Heads of numerous small, yellow-green flowers in umbels. Upright fleshy leaves. Perennial. Height to 45 cm. Jun-Aug.

On rocks around the coast. Occasionally on upper part of sand or shingle beach.

Leaves may be eaten raw or cooked and have a flavour similar to fennel but with a strong salty taste. When bruised or broken the leaves emit a distinct aroma of lemon oil. Rock Samphire was much used in Victorian times and has recently enjoyed a resurgence in popularity, often served with dishes including fish, quails eggs, sushi and salads. It is even used as a flavouring in alcoholic drinks such as Rock Samphire Gin.

Useful as a diuretic. It has a high vitamin C and mineral content and is thought to relieve flatulence and to act as a digestive remedy. It can also be brewed as a tea. Rock Samphire can purify the blood and remove toxins from the body. It is thought to be effective in a weight-loss diet.

This species can only be grown in coastal areas as it needs salt air and sea spray to acquire its distinctive flavour. Because of the perilous places where it grows it must be hand-picked. For these reasons restaurants can charge a premium. The parts gathered are the fresh young growth of the fleshy leaves and stems.

Family Apiaceae Fennel
(Foeniculum vulgare)   Ffenigl Cyffredin

Tall plant with large compound umbels composed of small yellow flowers. Leaves are very finely divided and smell of aniseed when crushed. Perennial. Height to 250cm. ❀ Jul-Oct.

Rocky places near the sea.

All parts of the plant are aromatic and used in flavouring foods particularly pastries, sweet pickles and fish.

Fennel has long been used as a common household remedy for a variety of complaints. These include the treatment of digestive problems including heartburn, intestinal gas, bloating, loss of appetite, and colic in infants. It has a diuretic effect which increases the amount and frequency of urination, thought to help remove toxic substances from the body. It is also regarded an effective herbal treatment for respiratory congestion and is a common ingredient in cough remedies. Fennel is often taken as a tea.

The seeds and oil extracted from Fennel smell and taste of aniseed and are used in soaps and perfumes. The dried leaves are believed to deter fleas from kennels and stables; when crushed are used as an insect repellent and as a flea repellent for dogs.

Family Apiaceae   Shepherd's-needle
(Scandix pecten-veneris)   Nodwydd y Bugail

Leaves are finely cut and the small white flowers are arranged in clusters (umbels) with 1-3 rays. The long, narrow and pointed fruits can reach up to 8cm in length. It is these structures that give it the common name. Annual. Height 15-50cm.

❀ May-Jul.

Critically endangered.

Coastal heathland near South Stack.

The young stem tips may be eaten raw or cooked.

Like many arable 'weed' species, the plant has declined in numbers as a result of changes in agricultural practices. A particular threat was stubble burning which was banned in the early 1990s. Since then there is evidence that the species has begun to recover in some areas of the UK. This plant is a UK Biodiversity Action Plan (UKBAP) priority species.

Family Apiaceae   Sea-holly
(Eryngium maritimum)   Celynen arfor

Bushy with spiny, blue-green holly-like leaves and pale veins. Flowers are grey-blue in colour and dome-shaped similar to a teasel rather than an umbellifer.

About the strandline on sandy shores; also shingle banks.

The young shoots are normally blanched by excluding light from the growing plant and are then used as an asparagus substitute. They are slightly sweet and smell of carrots. The boiled or roasted roots are said to resemble parsnips or chestnuts in flavour.

In the 17th and 18th centuries Sea-holly roots were collected on a large scale in England and were made into restorative lozenges. The plant is still used in modern herbalism and is valued especially for its diuretic properties.

A waxy covering on the leaves helps reduce transpiration in a windswept environment.

Family Asparagaceae Spring Squill
(Scilla verna)   Seren y Gwanwyn

Sometimes mistaken for a stunted Bluebell it bears spikes of up to 12 pale bluish-lilac flowers. With their short, strong stems they are ideally adapted to exposed wind-swept grassy cliffs. Perennial, growing from a bulb. Height 5-15 cm.

🌸 Apr-early Jun.

🔴

Coastal heathland and clifftops.

Family Asteraceae: Daisy family

The typical daisy flower is actually a composite head containing one or two types of small flowers called florets: outer ray florets (flat, often strap-shaped) and inner disc florets (tubular with 5 tooth-like lobes at the apex).

Each flower head sits in a cup, composed of overlapping scales called bracts.

Leaves are variable and may be simple or more occasionally compound, and their arrangement along the stem may be opposite, alternate or, less commonly, whorled.

The upper leaves are long and pointed whereas the lower leaves are lanceolate. It is the only dandelion type flower in the UK with grass like leaves. Each flower stem bears at the apex a single, large flower head, composed of golden-yellow florets. Annual to perennial. Height 30-80cm.

❀ Jun-Jul.

Sandy and calceareous soils. Dunes.

🍴 The young roots can be eaten raw whilst older roots are best cooked like parsnips. The roots have a sweet flavour due to their inulin content (inulins belong to a class of dietary fibres known as fructans). Young leaves and shoots may also be eaten raw or cooked and added to mixed salads or used in soups. The flowering stem, including the buds, can be cooked and served like asparagus.

📋 The plant has a number of medicinal uses including the treatment of liver and gallbladder problems. It appears to have a detoxifying effect and may stimulate the appetite and digestion. Its high inulin content makes this herb a useful food for diabetics since inulin does not raise blood sugar levels. A syrup made from the root may relieve coughs and bronchitis.

💅 The plant also has cosmetic properties. An infusion of the petals can clear the skin and lighten freckles. A distilled water made from the plant is used in cleansing lotions for dry skin.

Family Asteraceae South Stack Fleawort
(Tephroseris integrifolia subsp. maritima)

Has a rosette of leaves at the base with a single leafy stem bearing a few yellow, daisy-like flowers. It is a subspecies of the Field Fleawort. Biennial or short-lived perennial. Height 5-60cm.

May-Jun. Vulnerable (a schedule 8 plant protected species).

Found only on the grassy clifftops of South Stack. There are a handful of these plants growing on the cliff face near the RSPB Ellin's Tower but are too dangerously situated to view. Most are found a short walk away in an easterly direction where *Tephroseris integrifolia subsp. maritima* covers the steep cliffs, including the inaccessible cliff which projects into the sea.

Family Asteraceae Golden-samphire
(Inula crithmoides) Cedpwydd Suddlon

Succulent leaves having an aromatic scent and large, yellow, daisy-like flowers on long stems. Perennial. Height 15-80cm. Jul-Aug. Nationally scarce.

On rocks around the west coast. However, on sand in Newborough Warren.

Occasionally grown as a potherb. Young leaves may be eaten raw or cooked and the fleshy leaves and young shoots are pickled and used as a relish. In the past Golden Samphire was pickled in the same way as Rock Samphire but was considered inferior.

Family Asteraceae Sea Mayweed

(Tripleurospermum maritimum)   Amranwen Arfor

Large daisy-like flowers with yellow centres and white outer petals. The feathery leaves are finely divided. Perennial. Height to 60cm.
May-Sep.

On shingle banks, cliffs, the strandline.

When crushed the leaves yield a sweet smell similar to that of its relative, chamomile, though less pungent. It has antioxidant properties and is used to reduce skin inflammation and redness caused by daily stress.

Family Asteraceae Sea Aster
(Aster tripolium)   Seren y Morfa

A tall plant with fleshy leaves and flower heads of pale, bluish-purple but occasionally white.
Biennial. Height typically 50cm.

Jul-Oct.

Muddy salt marshes. Also coastal rocks and cliffs.

A tender succulent with a sweet, mild nutty flavour. The large leaves are also tender and delicious and may be cooked or pickled.

A halophyte which colonises areas frequently flooded by tides.

Family Asteraceae Cat's-ear
(Hypochaeris radicata) Melynydd

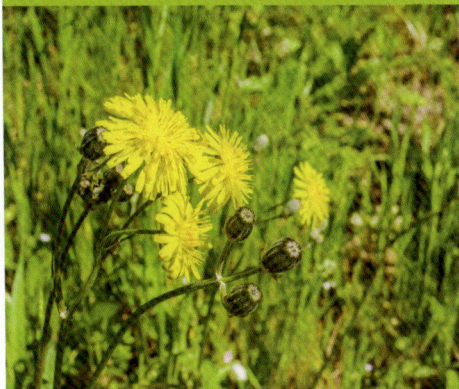

The long stems bear solitary, large yellow flower heads with numerous florets. The stem rises from a basal rosette of leaves. Perennial. Height 20-40 cm.

❀ Jun-Sep.

Dunes. Also old pastures and waste ground.

An aromatic plant which has traditionally been used for a wide variety of culinary purposes. It is rich in nutrients and antioxidants – hence its popularity in recipes around the world. All parts of the plant are edible. The leaves can be steamed and cooked as any other leafy vegetable and give flavour and texture to dishes such as stir-fries. The raw leaves can also be added to salads as can the petals which are also used to make wine. A ground coffee substitute is made from the roasted roots.

The plant has long been used for medicinal purposes. Uses include as a diuretic for kidney problems, and treating urinary infections, gallstones, rheumatism, constipation and liver problems.

Cat's-ear is considered harmful to livestock and horses. Ingestion of large amounts of the plant can cause a neurological disorder in horses called stringhalt, symptoms of which are involuntary twitching in the rear legs. Once the plant has been eliminated from the horse's diet the animal will gradually recover but this may take several years.

Family Asteraceae Smooth Cat's-ear
(Hypochaeris glabra) Melynydd Moel

A basal leaf rosette, often tinged reddish. One or more slender, leafless stems with solitary, yellow flower heads. Annual. Height 10-20cm. ❀ May-Sep. Vulnerable.

Fixed dunes. Also on bare ground and sparse grassland on poor, acidic, sandy soils.

The leaves may be eaten raw and are usually added to fresh garden salads. However, they can be steamed or boiled and used as soup or stew ingredients. The flowers, roots and stems may all be consumed. The root can also be used as a coffee substitute, being peeled, grated and roasted.

The whole plant is used in the treatment of wounds. The leaves are used to stem bleeding. The root is a mild laxative, diuretic and tonic.

Family Asteraceae Colt's-foot
(Tussilago farfara) Carn yr Ebol

Each stem has a solitary, yellow, daisy-like flower made up of numerous narrow rays surrounding central disc florets. The pinkish stems are covered in scales. Seeds possess hairs forming a 'clock'. Perennial. Height 5-15cm.

Feb-Apr.

Found generally. Bare ground on dunes. Shingle banks.

Flower buds and young flowers may be eaten raw or cooked. Having a pleasant aniseed flavour, they add a distinctive aromatic flavour to salads. Young leaves can be added to soups or cooked as a vegetable. An aromatic tea is made from the fresh or dried leaves and flowers and has a flavour similar to that of liquorice. The dried and burnt leaves are used as a salt substitute. The slender rootstock is candied in sugar syrup.

Despite serious safety concerns Colt's-foot is one of the most popular European remedies for the treatment of a wide range of chest complaints. The leaves are commonly used though the flowering stems are preferred in China. It is used to alleviate lung problems such as bronchitis, asthma and whooping cough and upper respiratory tract complaints including sore mouth and throat, cough and hoarseness. An extract prepared from the roots is used as an expectorant for the relief of coughs. Honey may be added to the flowers to make a cough syrup.

Rather like Dandelions, the seeds of a Colt's-foot flower form a 'clock' with each individual seed having its own hairy parachute, an effective method of wind dispersal. Seed heads of Colt's-foot were once used to stuff pillows.

Family Asteraceae Lesser Hawkbit
(Leontodon saxatilis) Peradyl Bach

Solitary, yellow
flower heads on
leafless unbranched
stems. Rosette of
leaves lying flat to
the ground.
Perennial. Height 8-
20cm. ✺ Jun-Oct.

Common in dune
slacks.

Family Asteraceae Sea Wormwood
(Artemisia maritima)   Wermod y Môr

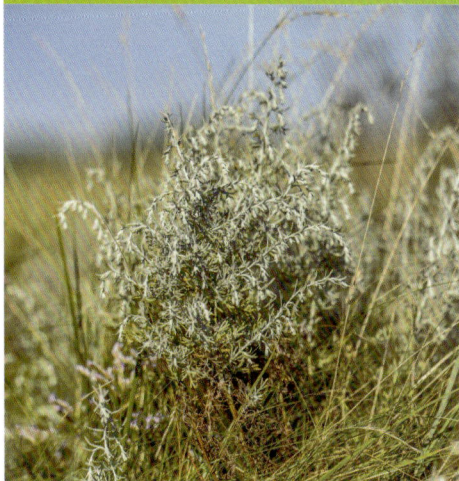

A deciduous strongly scented shrub. The leaves are narrow and covered on both sides with a coat of white cottony fibres. The small, inconspicuous flowers are yellow to brown. Perennial. Height 20-50cm. ✿ Aug-Sep.

Rocks above high water mark. Also shingle, drier areas of salt marshes.

Milder in its action than Wormwood *(A.absinthum)*, Sea Wormwood is used mainly as a tonic for the digestive system, in treating intermittent fevers and as an agent that destroys or expels parasitic worms.

The growing shoots are said to repel insects and mice and an infusion may discourage slugs.

Family Asteraceae   Carline Thistle
(Carlina vulgaris)   Ysgallen Siarli

While young and still in the bud stage the flower heads can be cooked and eaten like globe artichokes.

The plant is used as a remedy for colds, its root also serving as an effective diuretic. When applied externally it brings relief to various skin conditions such as acne and eczema. Carline Thistle contains the acetylide carlina oxide (furylbenzylacetylene), the main compound of the essential oil obtained from the plant. This chemical has a long history of medicinal use in Europe due to its anti-microbial properties. It is thought to be active against two strains of MRSA and a number of other resistant bacteria.

The flower head acts as a natural hygrometer as it is sensitive to the level of moisture in the air. It closes whenever the humidity rises above a certain point making it useful as a primitive weather forecasting device. A closed flower is taken as an indicator that rain is approaching. Foul smelling when freshly plucked from the ground, the root develops a pleasant aroma when dried.

An unattractive, spiny plant with distinctive brown and golden flower heads resembling thistles which have gone to seed although, in fact, they are in flower. It remains in bud for some time before the flower actually opens in July to August and by the end of September has completed flowering. Biennial. Height 10-60cm. ❀ Jul-Oct.

Sand dunes. Also grassy places on calcareous soil.

Family Boraginaceae Early Forget-me-not
(*Myosotis ramosissima*) Ysgorpionllys Cynnar

A slender, short, softly hairy plant with lance-shaped leaves in a rosette at the base. Un-stalked, oblong leaves on the stem. Small, bright blue flowers. Annual. Height 15-40cm. Apr-Jun.

On fixed dunes. Also thin soils over limestone. One of the first plants found flowering in the dunes in early spring.

Greyish-green downy leaves with drooping maroon-red flowers. Biennial. Height 30-60cm.
May-Jul. Near threatened.

Calcareous dunes. Also limestone grassland.

Hound's-tongue has a long history of use as a medicinal herb though it is rarely used in modern herbalism. The leaves contain allantoin, a highly effective agent that speeds up the body's healing process. The plant has been used internally in the treatment of coughs and diarrhoea. In modern medicine it is used mainly externally as a poultice on haemorrhoids, wounds, minor injuries, bites and ulcers.

Hound's-tongue contains alkaloids that are especially toxic to cattle and horses. The plant has a disagreeable odour and taste so is seldom eaten by animals but they may inadvertently eat the dried plant in hay. Sheep are more resistant than other livestock to the pyrrolizidine alkaloids.

Family Boraginaceae Viper's-bugloss
(*Echium vulgare*)   Tafod y Bwch

The leaves at the base are arranged in an upright rosette with bright blue, funnel-shaped flowers. Biennial. Height to 1 metre. ✿ Jun-Sep.

Sandy wasteland.

Viper's-bugloss was said to be an antidote to various poisons, in particular the venomous bite of a viper. The leaves and flowering stems may be used to relieve fevers, headaches, lung disorders, chest conditions, colds and nervous complaints.

Brassicaceae: Cabbage family
The flowers are cruciform (in the form of a cross) with four petals and four sepals.
The flowers are usually white, yellow or lavender.
Most are simple flowers with 4 long and 2 short stamens and a two-chambered ovary.
The leaves are mostly simple and alternately arranged.
The seeds are produced in dry pod-like fruits, often with a partition between the halves.

Family Brassicaceae Danish Scurvygrass
(Cochlearia danica)   Llwylys Denmarc

A delicate plant with numerous small, pale lilac flowers. Winter annual to biennial. Height 5-25cm. Feb-Jun.

Cliffs, walls and stony ground around the coast.

As it contains high levels of vitamin C the plant was once used to help prevent scurvy in sailors on long voyages.

A salt tolerant species. In recent times it has been found growing on verges alongside roads which have been treated with salt to prevent icing in winter, thus creating an ideal habitat.

- Has a basal rosette of pinnate leaves from which arise flowering stems bearing small, white flowers. Fruit is flattened, heart-shaped, notched at the tip. Winter-annual. Height 2-15cm.
- ❀ Mar-Jun. Near threatened.

- Dunes. Also shingle and heathland.

Family Brassicaceae   Wild Cabbage
(Brassica oleracea)   Bresych Gwyllt

Thick and fleshy leaves with large, pale yellow flowers. Perennial. Height 30-60cm.
May-Jul.
Nationally scarce.

Waste ground near the shore. Also sea cliffs.

The leaves may be eaten raw or cooked although taste slightly bitter when raw.

Has been used in the treatment of gout and rheumatism. The leaves can be used as a poultice to cleanse infected wounds - the midrib is removed and the leaf pressed with a warm iron then placed on the affected area. The seeds are diuretic, laxative and aid digestion.

The leaves form a rosette at the base of the plant. The small, white flowers are borne on single stems bearing few leaves. Narrow seed pods arranged in pairs. Annual. Height 2-30cm.

❀ Flowers throughout the year but particularly Apr-Jul.

Dunes.

The leaves have a mustard flavour and can be added to salads.

Used as a mouthwash.

A. thaliana is used in genetic engineering as a model plant for understanding the genetic, cellular, and molecular biology of flowering plants generally. It is the first plant to have its genome mapped and is the genetic reference plant for all other plant species. It has all the genes needed by more complex plants for characteristics such as root and seed production, genes that help repair cell walls and fight invading bacteria and fungi, and other medically useful genes, such as those responsible for glucosinolates (the chemical that gives cress its characteristically hot flavour).

Family Brassicaceae Sea-kale
(Cakile maritima) Hegydd Arfor

Grows in clumps of large purple-grey, cabbage-like leaves with small white flowers in dense flower heads. Perennial. Height 30-50cm. ✿ Late May-Jul.

On stable shingle and sand above high water mark.

All parts are edible. The tender shoots can be eaten raw or cooked much like asparagus. Young leaves may also be eaten raw or cooked like spinach. They have a pleasant almost nutty flavour and combine well in a mixed salad. The young flowering shoots are harvested before the flowers have opened. Used like sprouting broccoli, they are delicious when lightly steamed. Recently the plant has gained popularity in modern cuisine.

Family Brassicaceae Sea Rocket
(Cakile maritima) Hegydd Arfor

Waxy, thick lobed, green leaves with pale, lilac flowers. Annual. Height 15-50cms. Jun-Sep.

Sandy shores just above the strandline.

Leaves, stems, flower buds and immature seed pods may be eaten raw and have a strong, peppery flavour similar to horseradish or wasabi. The roots, resembling radishes, are also edible. The plant is rich in Vitamin C.

Low-growing plant with a basal rosette of narrow, pointed leaves from which arise slender stems bearing blue to deep blue scabious-like flower heads. Biennial. Height 5-30cm. ❀ May-Aug.

Dry banks, heaths and fixed dunes.

Caryophyllaceae: Campions, Carnations
Flowers usually white, pink or red with 5 sepals and 5 petals.
The 5 sepals may be joined, forming a tube.
Usually 5 or 10 stamens, with an ovary borne above them.
The ovules are located in the centre of the ovary.
Leaves in opposite pairs, un-lobed, un-toothed. Swollen leaf and stem joints.

Family Caryophyllaceae Sea Mouse-ear
(Cerastium diffusum)   Clust Llygoden Pedwar-gwryw

🌼 Small white flowers have 4 deeply notched petals with bases enclosed by green bracts. Hairy leaves often with purple fringing. Annual. Height 3-8cm. ❀ Mar-Jul.

🔴 Dunes and other sandy areas around the coast. Also shingle.

Family Caryophyllaceae Sea Sandwort
(Honckenya peploides) Tywodlys Arfor

A low-growing mat-forming plant with yellowish-green fleshy leaves and single white flowers. The plant has creeping runners that make it well adapted to growing in unstable pebbles. Perennial. Height 5-15cm. ✽ May-Jul.

Sandy beaches and shingle banks.

The young shoots contain high levels of vitamins A and C and have a delicious flavour eaten raw or cooked. The leaves can also be fermented and eaten like sauerkraut. In Iceland the plant is steeped in sour whey and allowed to ferment, the resulting liquor is said to taste similar to olive oil and is used as a beverage.

Family Caryophyllaceae Rock Sea-spurrey
(Spergularia rupicola) Tywodwlydd Y môrgreigiau

Has cylindrical fleshy leaves with small, lilac-pink flowers which are very sticky and hairy. Salt tolerant. Perennial. Height 5-15cm. ✳ Jun-Aug.

On rocks and cliffs around the coast.

Family Caryophyllaceae   Sea Campion
(Silene uniflora)   Gludlys Argor

Fleshy, waxy, grey-green leaves with abundant white flowers on short straight stems. Flowers are joined at their base to form a tube and surrounded by sepals forming a bladder-like structure. Perennial. Height 8-30cm. ❀ Apr-Aug.

Coastal cliffs, sand dune systems and gravel banks.

The tips of the foliage have a unique sweet flavour. Tender leaves should be cooked but can be eaten raw in small quantities.

Plants of the genus Silene have roots that contain the compound saponin which, although a mildly toxic substance, has long been used as soap for washing clothes. The Marbled Coronet Moth (Hadena confusa) lays its eggs in the seedpods.

Family Celastraceae Grass-of-Parnassus
(Parnassia palustris) Brial y Gors

Heart shaped basal leaves bear long stalks at the apex of which is a single white flower with five petals. Perennial. Height 10-30cm. ❀ Jul-Aug.

Dune slacks. Also marshes and fens.

The whole plant is astringent and slightly diuretic. A decoction is occasionally used as a mouthwash. The dried and powdered plant can be sprinkled onto wounds to aid the healing process. A distilled water made from the plant is an excellent astringent eye lotion.

This is not a grass at all! The name derives from Mount Parnassus in Greece where it grew abundantly on the slopes.

Family Cistaceae Spotted Rock-rose
(Tuberaria guttata subsp. breweri)

- The flowers are pale yellow with a dark crimson spot at the base of each petal. It flowers only once during its lifetime and sheds its vivid petals within hours of doing so. Annual. Height 2-15 cm. Jun-Aug. Near threatened.

- On dry heaths and coastal clifftops in a few places between Rhoscolyn and South Stack.

- The Spotted Rock-rose is Anglesey's county flower and is a locally rare species.
  Porth Diana in Trearddur Bay became a nature reserve in 1979 primarily to ensure the protection of the Spotted Rock-rose. This small reserve is part of the nationally important coastal heath on the west coast of Holy Island.

Family Convolvulaceae Sea Bindweed
(Calystegia soldanella)   Cynghafog Arfor

🌷 A prostrate plant with fleshy, round leaves and large, attractive, distinctive pink funnel-shaped flowers with five white stripes. Perennial. ❁ Jun-Aug.

🔴 Seaward edge of sand dunes.

🍴 The young shoots may be cooked as a vegetable or pickled and used as a Samphire substitute.

📔 Used to cure or prevent scurvy, as a diuretic and laxative, to reduce fever and to eliminate intestinal worms.

Family Convolvulaceae   Dodder
(Cuscuta epithymum) Llindag

Distinctive mats of thread-like stems with clusters of small, pale pink stalkless flowers. Annual. Height stems to 1m. ❀ Jun-Sep. Vulnerable.

Heathland and dune grassland. Found on Gorse and Heather.

When used in combination with other ingredients the seeds can assist with a variety of ailments. These include the treatment of infertility, osteoporosis, blood pressure, alopecia and urinary tract and liver disorders. The plant has anti-ageing and antioxidant properties and enhances the immune system.

Dodder has no roots and possesses only minute scale-like leaves. It lacks the plant pigment chlorophyll and so cannot make its own food by photosynthesis. It is a parasitic annual relying entirely on the host plant for its survival. The Dodder's stems attach to the host using small suckers which then penetrate the host's tissues and extract nutrients. The host plant is also used as a support and Dodder grows to forms mats over large Gorse bushes.

Family Cornaceae Yellow Bird's-nest
(Hypopitys monotropa) **Cyd-dwf**

An herbaceous plant of unusual appearance with yellow, waxy shoots lacking leaves. The downward drooping tubular flowers become erect in fruit. Perennial. Height 8-20cm. ☀ Jun-Aug. Endangered.

Found in dune slacks with Creeping Willow.

The plant is pale yellow as it lacks chlorophyll and cannot photosynthesise. It is frequently found growing under pines and this gave rise to its alternative common name, Pinesap. Recent research shows it to be epi-parasitic on the fungus of the genus *Tricholoma* that lives at the base of pine trees, using the fungus to extract nutrients and water from its host, the pine tree. Yellow Bird's-nest is able to live for years completely under the ground.

Family Crassulaceae   English Stonecrop
(Sedum anglicum)   Briweg y Cerrig

A low growing, evergreen succulent with short flower-bearing spikes. Small white star-shaped flowers tinged with pink on the outer edge of the petals. Perennial. Height 2-10cm.
Jun-Sep.

Rocky outcrops.

Succulents are plants with stems or leaves modified to become thickened and fleshy to retain water in arid climates. This colourful wild flower is now being used in 'green housing' where insulation is provided by plants that are allowed or actively encouraged to grow on roofs.
This method of roofing actually began many centuries ago in Iceland and the Faroe Islands. It gives insulation against the cold and the heat, repels rainwater and has the added advantage of sound proofing. As 'green living' is becoming more important, eco housing is gaining popularity throughout Europe.

Family Dipsacaceae Devil's-bit Scabious
(Succisa pratensis) Clafrllys Gwreidd-don

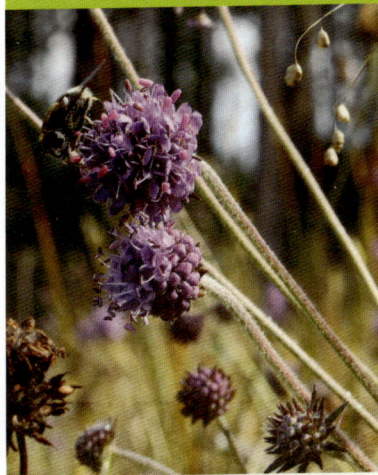

The plant has a basal rosette of lanceolate leaves which often have purplish blotches. Densely-packed compound flower heads sit on long stalks. Individual florets are four sided and deeply funnelled. Perennial. Height to 1m. ✽ Late Jun-Sep.

Damp, grassy areas. Rocky grasslands on calcareous to slightly acid soils.

The tender young shoots can be used as a salad ingredient.

Devil's-bit Scabious was used as a medicinal herb well into the 1900s but it is rarely used in modern-day herbal medicine. It was not only used to treat scabies but also for a number of ailments including poisonous insect bites, ringworm, thrush, intestinal worms, epilepsy, gonorrhoea and even the plague. Also as an external application to treat wounds, eczema and other skin conditions. The rootstock (rhizome) was the part mainly used. A preparation of distilled water treated conjunctivitis and a tincture was a gentle but reliable treatment for bruises. Some herbalists still use a decoction made from the rootstock to treat coughs, sore throat, bronchitis and fever.

The thick, glossy leaves were once used to dye wool green. The plant is the source of food for caterpillars of the Marsh Fritillary Butterfly (Euphydryas aurinia).

Ericaceae: The Heath family

Mostly shrubs (some herbs and trees).
The regular or nearly regular flowers typically have 5 sepals joined at the base.
Flowers have 5 petals usually united at the base and often in a bell shape.
Flowers are often urn-shaped with fused petals, white to pink or red in colour.
Usually 8 to 10 stamens and 1 ovary.
Leaves usually alternate, often evergreen.
The fruit is usually a berry or capsule.

Family Ericaceae   Heather
(Calluna vulgaris)   Grug

A low-growing evergreen with sprays of tiny, purplish-pink flowers. Height to 60cm.

Mid Jul-Sep.

Heaths, especially on outcrops of acidic rocks.

Traditionally, a type of brush was made by tying bunches of Heather to a handle to make a coarse broom for sweeping floors; they were standard household items in the days of 'dirt floors' and are still associated as 'witches' brooms. Other past uses of Heather include the dyeing of wool and leather tanning, bedding material for livestock and humans, for thatching roofs, as a fuel, in rope-making, and to repair holes in tracks and roads. It is still used as an ingredient in toiletries.

Family Ericaceae Bell Heather

(Erica cinerea) Clychau'r Grug

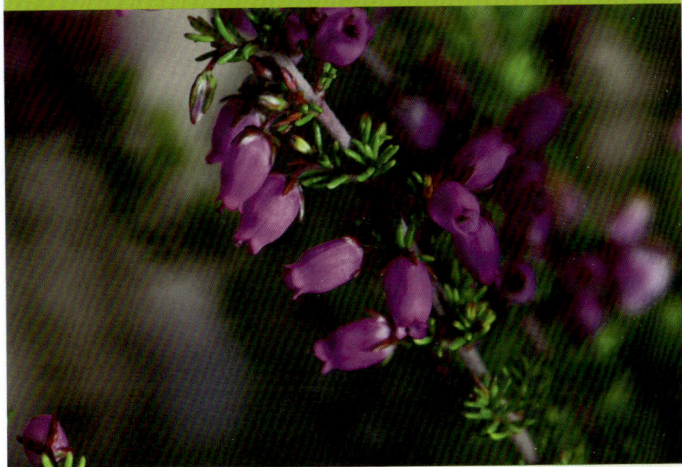

Distinctive dark purple-pink, bell-shaped flowers forming clusters around the stem with short, dark green needle-like leaves in whorls of three. The flowers are larger and brighter than *C. vulgaris* and appear slightly earlier in the summer. Height up to 60cm. ❀ Jun-Oct.

Drier parts of heaths and on outcrops of acidic rocks.

An important nectar source for all kinds of insects including Honeybees, Buff-tailed and Red-tailed Bumblebees, Ruby Tiger Moths and rare Silver-studded Blue Butterflies. The honey produced from bees feeding on Heather is dark and fragrant.

Family Ericaceae Cross-leaved Heath

(Erica tetralix) Grug Deilgroes

🌿 A bushy evergreen plant with leaves in a whorl of four, arranged up the woody stems. The plant has numerous heads of 8 to 10 rose pink, urn-shaped flowers. Height to 70cm. ✤ Jun-Sep.

🔴 Wet heaths.

Family Ericaceae Round-leaved Wintergreen
(Pyrola rotundifolia subsp. maritima) **Coed-wyrdd Crynddall**

Round, evergreen leaves and long-stalked stems with clusters of pale flowers towards the tip. Perennial. Height 10-30cm.

Jun-Sep. Nationally scarce.

Found in dune slacks.

A strong-smelling ingredient in many therapeutic liniments which are rubbed on various parts of the body to help ease muscle and joint pain.

The oil obtained from the leaves is used as flavouring in chewing-gum and toothpaste.

Family Euphorbiaceae: Spurges

The regular flowers are unisexual with male and female flowers usually borne on the same plant.

Flowers are distinctive and complex with neither male or female flowers having sepals or petals. The cluster of male and female flowers are in a cup-shaped cyathium.

These clusters of reduced flowers are enclosed by an involucre (whorl) of bracts that resembles flower petals.

The fruit is a three-chambered capsule.

Leaves are usually simple and are alternate (or, rarely, opposite or whorled) in arrangement along the stems. The stems of many species contain a milky white sap that can irritate the skin.

Family Euphorbiaceae   Portland Spurge
(Euphorbia portlandica)   GLlaethlys Portland

Consists of a cluster of leaves with yellowish bracts at the tip. The oval stem leaves are usually red as is the stem. The unusual cup-like flower heads lack petals and sepals. Biennial or short-lived perennial. Height 5-30cm.
✿ Apr-Sep.

Sand dunes. Also rocky and sandy places near the sea.

Members of the Euphorbia family typically produce a white, milky sap called latex that is relatively irritating to human skin. However, the sap has some degree of antifungal and antibacterial property and acts as an excellent wound sealant should the plant be damaged.

Family Euphorbiaceae Sea Spurge
(Euphorbia paralias) Llaethlys y Mor

🌺 A strange looking plant with straight, reddish stems and fleshy, grey-green leaves at the tip of which are small green complex 'flowers'. Perennial. Height 20-40cm. ☀ Jun-Sep.

🔴 Dunes and strandline of sandy beaches.

🟧 *Euphorbia paralias* is known in traditional medicine as an anti-inflammatory agent, as a purgative and for its local anaesthetic properties.

🟡 When damaged the leaves bleed an acrid white sap that can irritate the skin. Poachers used the poisonous sap extracted from stems of spurges to kill fish.

Family Fabaceae: Peas, Vetches & Clovers

Distinctive 5-petalled flower structure (2 lower petals fused to form a keel, 2 side petals form the wings, with a single standard upper petal).

The 5 sepals are usually fused into a tube.

Some have leaves modified as tendrils for support.

Fruit an elongated pod.

Family Fabaceae Narrow-leaved Vetch
(Vicia sativa subsp. nigra) Troellig arfor graig

A sprawling plant with tendrils for attachment. Pinkish-purple flowers. Leaflets on upper leaves much narrower than those on lower leaves. Annual. Height 15-150cm. ❀ May-Sep.

Dunes and nearby pastures.

The leaves when cooked have a flavour similar to that of peas. They can also be used as a tea substitute. The seeds can be dried, ground into a powder and mixed with cereal flour to make bread, biscuits and cakes.

All members of this family are able to fix nitrogen and may be used as a fallow or meadow crop. Also useful as livestock fodder.

Family Fabaceae Hop Trefoil
(Trifolium campestre)   **Meillionen Hopys**

🌼 Short, hairy, erect plant. The trifoliate leaflets are slightly serrated, oval, narrowing towards the base; the central one is short stalked. The yellow flowers resemble miniature pea flowers packed densely into round or oval heads. Annual. Height 10-30cm. ❀ May-early Oct.

🔴 Common on dunes.

🍴 The dried flower heads can be ground into a flour. It was used to make bread in times of famine.

Family Fabaceae Common Restharrow

(Ononis repens) **Tagaradr**

Low growing, clump-forming plant having sticky leaves divided into three oval leaflets. Hairy stems and clusters of small, pink, pea-like flowers. Perennial. Height 10-60cm. ❁ Jun-Sep.

Fixed dunes.

The root may be eaten raw as a liquorice substitute. Soaked in cold water it makes a refreshing cold drink. The young shoots were at one time much used as a vegetable, being boiled, pickled or eaten in salads.

The whole plant has been used in the treatment of bladder stones and to subdue delirium. It was once widely used in Russian herbal medicine.

Oval heads of pale pink flowers covered in soft hairs giving it the downy appearance of the paw of a rabbit or hare. Narrow, oval leaflets toothed at the tip. Annual. Height 5-20cm. ❀ Jun-Sep.

Abundant on sand dunes.

Used in the treatment of diarrhoea.

Family Fabaceae Common Bird's-foot-trefoil
(Lotus corniculatus)   Pys y Ceirw

A low sprawling plant with yellow to orange or red tinged flowers in clusters at tips of the stalk. Perennial. Height 10-50cm. ✿ May-Sep.

Grassland, heaths and dunes.

Bird's-foot-trefoil was incorporated into the protective wreaths of golden flowers worn on Midsummer Night (known as Herb Evening). It's trifoliate leaves link to the Trinity, while the horn-like seed pods allude to the devil. Trefoil is believed to be the incarnation of Tom Thumb (a tiny man) as the leaves resemble the Devil's fingers.
Used in agriculture as a forage plant, grown for pasture, hay, and silage.

Family Fabaceae Kidney Vetch
(Anthyllis vulneraria)   Plucen Felen

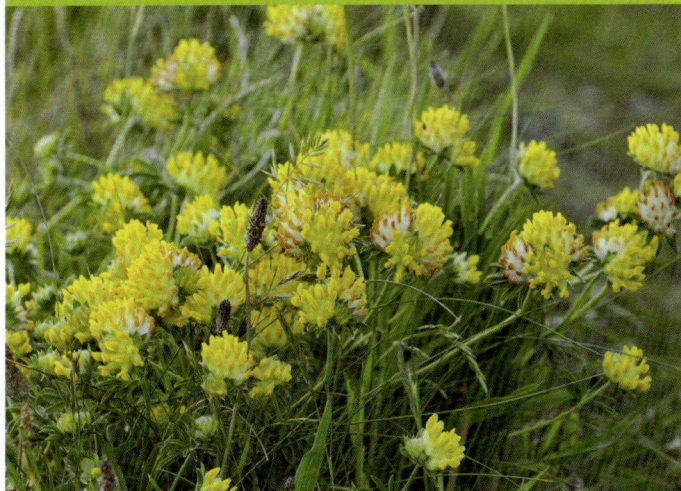

🌼 Large, kidney-shaped flower heads, which may be yellow, orange or occasionally red. Upper leaves have pairs of leaflets with one terminal leaflet. Perennial. Height to 60cm. ❀ May-Sep.

📍 Dunes and cliffs around the coast.

💊 Externally applied, the plant was an ancient remedy for skin eruptions, minor wounds, cuts and bruises. Internally it was used as a treatment for constipation and as a tonic. Kidney Vetch was also once given as a remedy for kidney disorders and is also sometimes used in cough-relieving teas.

🐛 The plant provides food for a number of beetle and moth larvae but, most importantly, is the sole food plant for the caterpillars of the rare Small Blue Butterfly, *Cupido minimus*.

Family Fabaceae Gorse
(Ulex europaeus) Eithinen Ffrengig

A very spiny, evergreen shrub with densely packed yellow, coconut scented flowers, in bloom for much of the year. Height to 3m.
❀ Jan-Dec.

Rough grassland, scrub, cliffs, open heathland, usually on acid soils.

The flower buds can be pickled in vinegar and then used like capers. A tea is made from the shoot tips.

Gorse flowers have been used in the treatment of jaundice and as a treatment for scarlet fever in children.

Gorse was at one time used as an under-thatch on Welsh cottages beneath the final layer of straw. It was also used as a fuel, notably in bakers' ovens. The ashes made an excellent soil dressing. Another use for the alkali-rich ashes was as a detergent in washing, either in the form of a solution or mixed with clay and made into balls, as a substitute for soap. Gorse seeds were soaked and used as a flea repellent.

Family Fabaceae   Western Gorse
(Ulex gallii)   Eithinen Man

- Similar to *U.europaeus* but smaller and more delicate. Height 30–100cm.
- Mid Jul–Oct.

- Dry heaths.

Family Frankeniaceae Sea-heath
(Frankenia laevis) Rhostir môr

Mat-forming with distinct, evergreen stalkless leaves and delicate pink flowers with 5 petals. Perennial. Height to 35cm.
Jun-Sep. Near threatened.

Upper zone of sandy salt marsh. (Often in the transition between salt marsh and sand dunes.)

Frankenia is the only genus in the Frankeniaceae family.

Gentianaceae: Gentian family

The family consists of trees, shrubs and herbs showing a wide range of colours and floral patterns.

Regular flowers with distinctive, bell-shaped blossoms.

Flowers have 4 or 5 separate sepals, 4 or 5 united petals and 4 or 5 stamens.

Leaves are mostly opposite, often lacking petioles (leaf stalks) and have smooth margins.

The ovary matures as a capsule with many seeds.

Family Gentianaceae   Lesser Centaury
(Centaurium pulchellum) Canri Leiaf

Has narrow 3-7 veined leaves which grow in opposite pairs along the stems. It has small, bright pink 5-petalled flowers borne in loose clusters at the tips of the pale green stalks.
Annual. Height 2-15cm. Jun-Sep.

Dunes and upper salt marsh.

Centaury contains bitter substances used medicinally in earlier times. Gentian extracts from many species have been shown to be anti-inflammatory, antifungal, and also reduces fevers. As a result it has been used to treat a wide variety of ailments.

Family Gentianaceae Autumn Gentian
(Gentianella amarella) Crwynllys Chwerw

A short and well branched plant with dark green, linear leaves. Bell-shaped purple flowers. Biennial. Height 3-30cm. ☀Jul- Oct.

Sand dunes. Also disused limestone quarries.

Gentian has a long history of use in the treatment of digestive disorders. It is especially useful in states of exhaustion from chronic disease and in all cases of debility, weakness of the digestive system and lack of appetite. Today, gentian root is used specifically to protect the liver, stimulate its function, help regenerate the cells and increase the flow of bile. The plant is used in Bach Flower Remedies.

Family Gentianaceae Yellow-wort
(Blackstonia perfoliata) Canri Felen

The oval triangular leaves are distinctive and enclose the stem. The flowers have sepals almost cut to the base and 6-8 yellow petals forming a short tube. Annual or biennial. Height 15-50cm.
❁ Jun-Oct.

Sand dunes.

A yellow dye is obtained from the plant extract.

Family Gentianaceae Seaside Centaury
(Centaurium littorale) Canri Goch Arfor

Has a basal rosette of narrow leaves and tips resembling spoons. From these arise straight stems, singly or in twos or threes with vivid pink, funnel-shaped flowers, stalk-less at the apex. Biennial. Height to 25cm.

Jul-Aug.

Nationally scarce.

Rare on dunes of Newborough Warren and Aberffraw Common.

Geraniaceae: Geranium family - Cranesbills and Storksbills

Regular flowers with 5 separate sepals and 5 separate petals with 5, 10 or 15 stamens.

The leaves are alternate or opposite. The leaf blades are lobed or compound. They have a small appendage or stipule just beneath the point where they attach to the stem.

In Cransesbills the leaves are palmately-lobed, with the main veins radiating from a central point at the tip of the stalk. In Storksbills the leaves are pinnately-lobed, with the main veins radiating from the central vein.

After pollination the seed pods are extended to form a needle-like structure (often referred to as a 'beak') emerging from the centre of the flower.

Family Geraniaceae Bloody Crane's-bill
(Geranium sanguineum)   Pig yr Aran Rhuddgoch

Leaves are long-stalked, deeply divided into 5 to 7 lobes with large, solitary, crimson flowers. Perennial. Height 10-40. ✽ May-Aug.

Dry banks, cliff tops and dunes.

The leaves and flowers can be brewed into a tea.

The oil of the Geranium makes a good astringent and can be diluted with water and used topically to cleanse the face or be added to a bath. It also has antiseptic properties and is said to help restore the balance of dry or oily skin and hair. Recently the antiviral properties of extracts from *G.sanguineum* have been the subject of scientific research.

Family Geraniaceae Common Stork's-bill
(Erodium cicutarium)   Pig y Crëyr Cegidaidd

Low-growing plant with finely-cut leaves and small, pink flowers. Seed pods are extended as a distinctive 'beak'. Annual. ✿ Apr-Sep.

Sand dunes. Also sandy pastures.

The young tender leaves and stems may be eaten raw and added to salads as they have a similar taste to parsley.

The root and leaves are the main parts used in traditional medicine; breast-feeding mothers eat these to increase their milk flow. In Mexico the plant was used to control bleeding and prevent infection following childbirth. Externally the decoction of the root is used as an antidote to insect bites and to soothe the associated pain. It is also useful for skin infections. In the past an infusion was given as a remedy for typhoid fever. It has astringent and antioxidant properties. In Peru it is used by traditional healers to regulate blood pressure. In the well-known Bach Flower Remedies *E.cicutarium* is thought to relieve obsessive anxiety or worrying.

Lamiaceae: Mint family

Many plants in the mint family form dense mats or clumps.

Flowers often grow in closely packed whorls around their stems.

Flowers are typically two-lipped. The upper lip forms a hood, while the lower lip acts as a landing platform for visiting insects.

Stems are always square.

Leaves arranged in opposite pairs.

Family Lamiaceae Selfheal
(Prunella vulgaris) Craith Unnos

🌺 A short, creeping plant with square stems and bright green oval leaves, found in opposite pairs. The violet flowers are hooded and two lipped, arranged into a slightly oblong dense head. Perennial. Height to 20cm. ❀ Jun-Sep.

📍 Dune slacks. Also on damp grassland.

🍴 The young leaves and stems can be eaten raw in salads. Also used in soups and stews or boiled as a potherb giving a subtle bitter taste. The aerial parts of the plant can be powdered and brewed in a cold infusion to make a beverage.

❗ Selfheal has been used as an alternative medicine for centuries for many ailments in many parts of the world. A weak infusion of the plant is an excellent eye wash for styes and conjunctivitis. A decoction of the leaves is used to treat sore throats and a medicinal tea given in the treatment of fevers, diarrhoea, internal bleeding and weaknesses of the liver and heart. It may be used in alternative medicine as an antibiotic and anti-inflammatory. Can be applied externally for treating minor injuries, sores, burns and bruises.

Family Lamiaceae Wild Thyme
(Thymus polytrichus)   Gruwlys Gwyllt Mwaf

Occurring in dense mats. Short erect stems bear rounded heads of purple flower heads composed of many small flowers. The stems are square and hairy on 2 opposite sides. Perennial.
Height to 10cm. ❁ May-Sep.

Dunes. Also dry limestone soils, heaths and cliff tops.

Its fragrant scent and taste provide a flavoursome seasoning particularly for poultry and pork.

Thyme oil is one of the strongest antioxidants known and has been used as a medicinal herb since ancient times. It contains thymol which acts as a digestive tonic and mild antiseptic. It is used as a mouthwash and brewed as an herbal tea. In the past sprigs were placed under the pillow to aid sleep and posies of Wild Thyme were used to ward off infectious diseases.

Red and White Thyme oils are used in perfumes, soaps and cosmetics.

Family Lentibulariaceae Common Butterwort
(Pinguicula vulgaris) Toddyn Cyffredin

One to three slender stems are produced from a rosette of greenish-yellow leaves that lie flat to the ground. At the apex of each stem is a violet-blue flower. Perennial. Height 5-18cm.
❀ May-Jul.

Found in dune slacks. Also bogs and fens.

Once used to curdle milk and in Scandinavia is still used for this purpose. The milk is poured over a strainer on which fresh leaves of Butterwort have been laid. The milk is then left for a day or two until it sours and solidifies to the consistency of yoghurt.

Butterwort is little used in contemporary herbal medicine though it was once commonly prepared in Wales as a laxative. A tea brewed from the leaves was taken to relieve whooping cough and other respiratory diseases. The leaves, used externally as a poultice, were applied to wounds to aid the healing process and to eliminate warts. Also used as a remedy for skin rashes, eczema, ringworm, insect bites and stings.

In folklore it was believed that when cows' udders were rubbed with Butterwort leaves the cows were protected from evil spirits resulting in especially enriched milk and butter. Butterwort is able to thrive on poor, permanently wet, acidic soil. The plant is insectivorous and survives by feeding on insects which become trapped when they land on the sticky leaves. In attempting to escape, the insect stimulates the leaf to curl around it and digestive enzymes are released. The resultant digested liquid is absorbed by the leaf.

Family Linaceae Fairy Flax
(Linum catharticum) Llin y Tylwyth Teg

Fine, low-growing stems bearing small white flowers with five petals. Leaves opposite, oblong to lanceolate with one vein. Annual or biennial. Height 5-25cm. ❀ May-Sep.

Sand dunes. Also on basic soils in limestone areas.

Seldom used in modern herbalism, the plant was once popular as a gentle laxative and also for the treatment of muscular rheumatism, liver complaints, jaundice and catarrhal problems. It was harvested in the summer when first flowering and dried for later use.

Orchidaceae: Orchid family

A family with distinctive, complex flowers.
All orchids have the same flower structure with 3 sepals and 3 petals.
The sepals may be green or coloured like the petals.
The lower petal (known as the lip) differs in size and shape from the other petals.
The lip may be very elaborate, and in many orchids is extended back into a tubular spur.
The filaments, anthers, style and stigma are reduced in number and are usually fused into a single structure called the column.
The ovary matures as a 3-valved capsule with numerous minute seeds.

Family Orchidaceae Early Marsh-orchid
(Dactylorhiza incarnata) Tegeirian y Gors

Numerous small, deep red flowers in crowded spikes. Perennial. Height 20-40cm. ✿ Late May-Jun.

Grows profusely in the dune slacks of Newborough Warren. Also frequent in base-rich marshes and fens. There are several subspecies which differ in flower colour.

The root bulb may be cooked and is very nutritious. It is a source of 'salep', a fine yellowish-white powder obtained by drying the tuber and grinding it into a powder. Salep is a starch-like substance with a sweetish taste and a rather unpleasant smell. It is made into a drink or can be added to cereals and used in bread making. 25g of salep is said to be enough to sustain a person for a day.

Salep may be used as a demulcent (relieves irritation of the mucous membranes in the mouth). Because of its high nutritional value it was added to the diets of convalescents.

In the middle of summer the Early Marsh-orchid exploits the general lack of flowers in damp habitats and Bumblebees are attracted by their colourful, though nectar-less, flowers. The flower is also visited by flies and beetles. Although found widely throughout the UK it is increasingly marginalised due to wetland drainage and destruction of habitat for agricultural purposes causing serious decline in some habitats. The Early Marsh-orchid grows exclusively in damp calcareous areas. The dune system is an ideal habitat where fragmented seashells produce a soil with a high calcium content and the dune slacks, which are submerged in rainwater during winter and early spring, retain high levels of moisture throughout the year.

Family Orchidaceae Marsh Helleborine
(Epipactis palustris) Caldrist y Gors

Each single, tall erect stem bears distinctive clusters of triangular shaped flowers which are either brownish-purple or creamy-green. The white lip of each flower is 'frilly' in appearance. Perennial. Height 20-45cm
Late Jun-early Aug.

Abundant in dune slacks. Also fens and base-rich marshes.

Marsh Helleborine thrives in habitats which are usually submerged during the winter and maintain high levels of moisture during the summer. Thus dune slacks provide an ideal habitat as do the Anglesey fens which are fed by alkaline springs running through limestone rocks.

Family Orchidaceae Early Marsh-orchid
(Epipactis dunensis) Caldrist y Twyni

Dune Helleborine has both pale yellow-green leaves and flowers, the latter with faintly tinged pink petals. Perennial. Height 20-50cm.
❀ Late Jun-mid Aug. Rare.

Among Dwarf Willow in dune slacks of Newborough Warren. Also in the adjacent forest area where specimens are much taller as they are more sheltered from the effect of strong winds than in exposed sand dunes.

Family Orchidaceae Common Twayblade
(Neottia ovata) Ceineirian

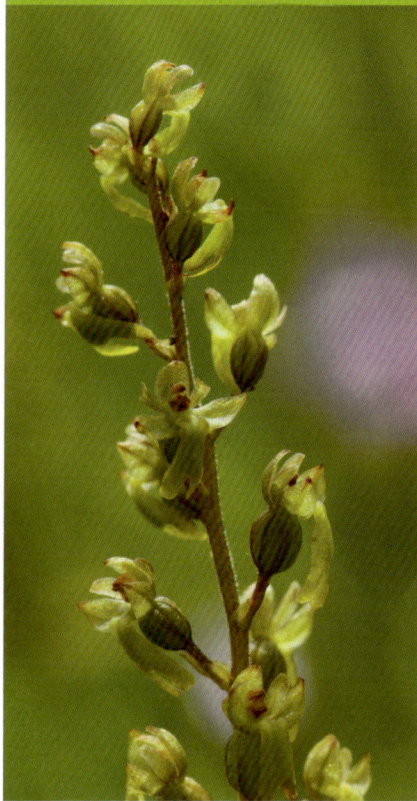

An inconspicuous orchid as the flowers, stems and leaves are all green. 'Twa blades' or two blades is the origin of the common name of this wild orchid and refers to the single pair of opposite leaves at the base of the flowering stem. The long, slender flower spike is distinctive with as many as 100 separate small, green flowers. Perennial. Height 20-60cm. ✿ Late Apr-Jun.

Found in dune grassland. Also in woods and around fens.

In ancient times the flowers were incorporated in ointments to heal wounds.

One of the first orchids to be recognised in Britain. It is now very widespread throughout the country and grows in many habitats.

Family Orchidaceae Pyramidal Orchid
(Anacamptis pyramidalis) Tegeirian Bera

An erect orchid bearing bright-pinkish flowers which are first pyramid shaped but once fully developed become cylindrical. Perennial. Height 20-60cm.

Early Jun-mid Jul.

Dune slacks. Also calcareous grassland.

The dried and ground tuber, which should be harvested as the plant dies down after flowering and setting seed, gives a fine white powder called salep. This very nutritious sweet and starch-like substance is used in drinks, cereals and for making bread.

Salep is also incorporated in diets for children and convalescents, being boiled with water, flavoured and prepared in the same way as arrowroot.

The Bee Orchid has distinctive flowers with three bright pink sepals. The petals are green or pinkish-brown and are much smaller and narrower than the sepals. In the centre of the flower the stamens and stigmas have fused to form a column. Usually 3 to 5 flowers are produced but more robust specimens may have as many as 10 flowers. Each flower closely resembles a bumblebee in appearance. Perennial. Height 10-45cm. ✿ Jun-early Jul.

Sand dunes. Also dry, calcareous pastures.

The Bee Orchid is self-pollinated. Other species of the genus Ophrys, such as the Early Spider and Fly Orchids, have an elaborate pollination mechanism. Newly emerged male bees are attracted by 'false pheromones' emitted by the orchids. They attempt to copulate with the flower and in so doing pick up pollen which is subsequently transferred to the next flower visited.

Family Orchidaceae Autumn Lady's-tresses
(Spiranthes spiralis) Ceineirian Troellog

A slender plant with small white scented flowers that spiral around the stem from near the base to the apex. Sepals and petals form a trumpet. The blue-green leaves cling to the stem and have the appearance of scales. The lower flowers open first and are often fading before the uppermost flowers have opened. Perennial. Height 3-20cm. Aug-Sep. Near threatened.

In short turf on calcareous soils, coastal flat-topped cliffs and dunes.

A tincture of the root has been prepared as a homeopathic remedy used in the treatment of skin conditions, painful breasts, kidney pain and eye complaints.

Orobanchaceae: Broomrape family

The regular flowers grow either in spikes or singly at the apex of the slender stem.
The 2-5 sepals are united to form a tube and there are 5 joined petals.
The petals may be yellowish, brownish, purplish or white.
The upper lip is two-lobed, the lower lip is three-lobed.
There are 4 stamens, 2 long and 2 short.

Family Orobanchaceae Confused Eyebright
(Euphrasia confusa) Effros Gliniog

🌷 Small, serrated leaves, mostly opposite. Tiny white to purple flowers. Annual. Height 2-20cm.
 ❁ May-Sep.

📍 Heaths and dune grassland. Also old pastures and meadows.

🍴 Used as a flavouring ingredient.

👆 A hemi-parasite of low fertility grasslands, particularly dry habitats on calcareous soils. The plants parasitise and draw nutrients from the roots of a wide range of meadow plants including grasses and legumes.

Family Orobanchaceae Red Bartsia
(Odontites vernus) Gorudd

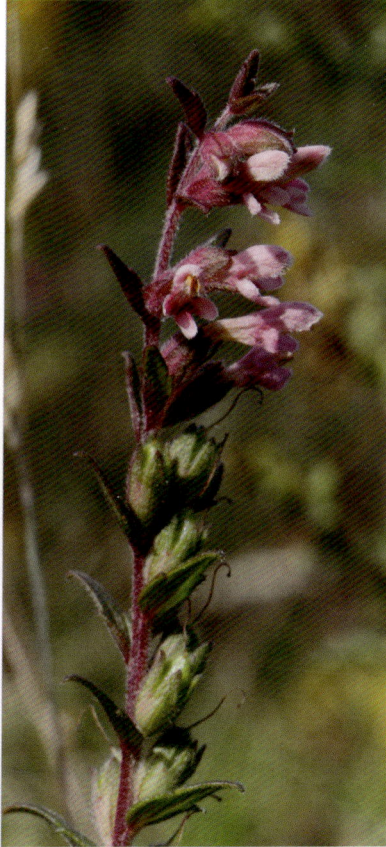

Slender erect stems with spikes of small reddish-pink flowers with 4 petals and 4 sepals. Leaves are simple and opposite, the upper leaves intersperse the flowers. Easily overlooked especially when growing among tall grass. Annual. Height to 30cm. ❀ Jun-Sep.

Rocky seashores and upper zones of salt marshes. Also on low fertile soils.

Red Bartsia was once used as cure for toothache, hence the genus name 'odons' which is Greek for 'tooth'.

Red Bartsia is a hemi-parasite, gaining extra nutrients from the roots of its nearby host grasses. It attaches onto the roots of the grasses and takes water and minerals from them. Popular with Common Carder Bees; one particular species *(Melitta tricincta)* feeds solely on Red Bartsia.

Family Orobanchaceae   Yellow Bartsia
(Parentucellia viscosa) Gorudd Melyn

A stiff, slender unbranched stem coated in hairs and sticky glands bearing opposite leaves and bright yellow flowers. Hemi-parasite. Annual. Height 10-50cm. ✸ Jun-Oct.

Grassy places on damp sandy soil near the sea.

Family Orobanchaceae   Yellow-rattle
(Rhinanthus minor)   Cribell Felen

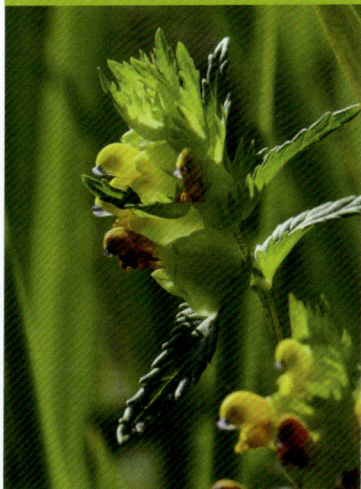

Has yellow, two lipped flowers, the upper lip having two white or purple 'teeth'. Behind the flower the joined sepals inflate to form a green bladder occasionally tinged red. The opposite, simple leaves have serrated margins and deep dark green veins. Annual. Height to 50cm.
✿ May-Sep.

Dune grassland.

The plant is used by conservationists to promote biodiversity of meadows i.e. to turn improved grassland back to meadow. Through feeding off the vigorous grasses, Yellow-rattle eventually allows more delicate, traditional species to colonise. Yellow-rattle is a root hemi-parasite of a wide range of meadow plants especially grasses and legumes. Whilst capable of carrying out its own photosynthesis it is dependent upon these hosts for additional supplies of carbohydrates and minerals. By drawing nutrients from surrounding vegetation it limits their growth and helps maintain an open grassland. Following flowering the seed capsule rattles within the brown papery bladder. It was believed to indicate that the hay meadow was ready to be cut hence its other common name of Hay-rattle.

The ripening seeds of Yellow-rattle provide the only food source for the larvae of the moth, Grass Rivulet (Perizoma albulata). This moth is mainly found in calcareous grasslands, dune slacks and coastal shingle.

Family Orobanchaceae English Eyebright
(Euphrasia officinalis subsp. anglica) Effros Lloegr

The tiny white to purple flowers have dark veins; the upper petals are two-lipped and the lower single lip is split into three lobes. The small leaves are toothed. Annual. Height 2-25cm.
May-Sep.

Dune grassland and heaths.

Eyebright herb tea contains several minerals and chemicals that can combat bacteria, specifically those that attack the eye in problems such as conjunctivitis. Eyebright has been used in alternative medicine as an aid in treating nasal congestion, sinus pain, cough, breathing problems and the common cold. However, research has failed to prove its effectiveness.

Family Papaveraceae Yellow Horned-poppy
(Glaucium flavum) Pabi Corniog Melyn

A straggly coastal plant with golden yellow flowers which appear in June and are followed by the 'horns', curling seedpods that can be up to 30cm long. When damaged the plant exudes a poisonous yellow sap. Biennial to perennial. Height to 90cm.

Jun-Sep.

Local and scarce on shingle banks.

The seed oil contains glaucine, an alkaloid that can be used in cough medicines. The plant was at one time applied to bruises.

In the past oil produced from the seeds of Yellow Horned-poppy was used to make soap. The oil was also burned in lamps.

Family Plumbaginaceae   Thrift
(Armeria maritima) Clustog Fair

The densely-packed short, grass-like leaves form rounded cushions from which pink flowers in compact inflorescence are borne on long, thin, leafless stalks. Perennial. Height 5-30cm.
❁ Late Apr-Jul.

Rocks and dry banks around the coast. Also salt marshes.

Thrift is rarely used in herbal medicine, though the dried flowering plant is reputed to have antibiotic properties and has been used in the treatment of obesity, some nervous disorders and urinary infections.

The plant is copper tolerant and is able to grow in soils with copper concentrations of up to 6400 mg/kg.

Family Plumbaginaceae Rock Sea-lavender
(Limonium binervosum agg.) Llemyg y Mor-greigiau

- A delicate plant with compact rosette of strap-shaped leaves from which arise fine, branched flowering stems bearing numerous spikes of attractive bluish-lilac coloured flowers. Perennial. Height 8-30cm. ❁ Jul-Sep.

- On sea cliffs. Occasional on drier, upper salt marshes.

- It belongs to a group of nine closely related species which are very similar in appearance and difficult to identify. Despite the common name, Rock Sea-lavender is not related to the Lavender. Over-picking of Sea-lavender has occurred in some areas because of its popularity in floral decorations.

Family Plumbaginaceae   Lax-flowered Sea-lavender
(Limonium humile)

🌿 Easily confused with Common Sea-lavender which has broader leaves and flowers that are more clustered together. The stems of Lax-flowered Sea-lavender are often angular. Perennial. Height to 40cm. ❀ Jul-Aug. Nationally scarce.

🔴 Firm muddy salt marshes.

🍃 Very difficult to identify. Hybrids with Common Sea-lavender can occur. Can also be confused with Rock Sea-lavender which is very variable being split into 22 slightly differing plants: 6 species and 16 subspecies, mostly identifiable only by experts and by specific location. Lax-flowered Sea-lavender can only be accurately identified by microscopic examination of the pollen.

Family Polygalaceae   Heath Milkwort
(Polygala serpyllifoli) Llysiau'r Groes

Similar to *P. vulgaris* (Common Milkwort) but the lower leaves are usually opposite rather than alternate and the flower colours are often a deeper shade. The flowers are usually blue but pink and white flowers do occur. Perennial. Height to 15cm.

May-Sep.

Heaths and acidic soils.

Family Polygonaceae Curled Dock
(Rumex crispus subsp. littoreus) Tafol Crych

🌷 The basal leaves form a rosette from which the flowering stalk arises. The leaves are narrow and strap-shaped with distinctive waved or curled edges. The inflorescence is much branched. Each yellowish or reddish green flower lacks petals and consists of 3 inner sepals and 3 outer sepals. The fruiting stem has large warts on the sepals. Perennial. Height 50-120cm. ❀ May-Oct.

🔴 The main dock in the dunes. Also shingle banks and the fringes of salt marshes.

🍴 The leaves can be added to salads or soups and cooked as a potherb. Only the very young leaves should be used, preferably before the stems have developed. The leaves are very rich in vitamins A and C and minerals, especially iron. Stems, raw or cooked, are best peeled and the inner portion eaten. Raw or cooked seeds can be ground into a powder and used as a flour. A coffee substitute can be prepared from the roasted seeds.

📋 Curled Dock has a long history of domestic herbal use. All parts can be used, though the root is most effective medicinally. It is a gentle and safe laxative. Externally, the root can be mashed and used as a poultice and salve, or dried and used as a dusting powder on sores, ulcers, wounds and other skin problems.

Family Primulaceae Bog Pimpernel
(Anagallis tenella) Gwlydd y Gors

Creeping stems with pairs of heart shaped leaves at regular intervals. The small, lilac-pink lightly-veined, bell-shaped flowers grow singly on short upright stalks. The flowers usually have 5 to 7 petals, backed by pointed short sepals. Extremely fragile, the plant is likely to break when handled.
Perennial. Height to 20cm.
✿ May-Sep.

Dune slacks. Also bogs.

Family Primulaceae   Brookweed
(Samolus valerandi) Claerlys

Spoon-shaped, pale green leaves in the form of a basal rosette. The flower spike bears small, white, bell-shaped flowers towards the apex. The flowers have 5 petals and 5 sepals. Perennial. Height to 45cm.
Jun-Aug.

Dune slacks.

The young leaves have a rather bitter taste but may be eaten raw or cooked.

As it has a high vitamin C content it may be eaten to prevent scurvy. The plant was often used to heal wounds, rashes and ringworm and also as an astringent and a laxative.

Family Ranunculaceae Lesser Meadow-rue
(Thalictrum minus) Arianllys Bach

The tiny green, yellow or purple-tinged drooping flowers are carried on narrow stems above the leaves which are divided into many small leaflets. The flowers lack petals but have 4-5 sepals. Perennial. Height 25-120cm. ❀ Jun-Aug.

Sand dunes.

An infusion of the leaves, or a decoction of the root, is used in the treatment of fevers.

Family Ranunculaceae Bulbous Buttercup
(Ranunculus bulbosus) Chwys Mair

The attractive, shiny yellow flowers with 5-7 petals form at the apex of the stems. It has downturned sepals beneath the petals. The three-lobed basal leaves are deeply divided. Perennial. Height 15-40cm.

Late Mar-early Jun.

Fixed dunes. Also limestone grassland.

Despite serious safety concerns all parts of the plant are used to treat skin diseases, arthritis, gout, nerve pain and influenza. All members of the Ranunculaceae family contain the toxic glycoside ranunculin. It is avoided by livestock when fresh but when the plant dries the toxin breaks down, so hay containing the plant is safe for animal consumption.

Family Rosaceae Tormentil
(Potentilla erecta) Tresgl y Moch

The stems are slender and richly branched. The shiny, dark green leaves are alternate and consist of three leaflets with serrated margins. Each flower stalk produces one single yellow flower at the tip. The flower has four petals (most plants in the genus Potentilla have five) which form a cross-like shape. Perennial. Height 10-30cm. ❀ May-Sep.

Rough pastures and heaths.

The medicinal uses of Tormentil have been known for centuries. The whole plant, but especially the rootstock (rhizome), has antibiotic properties and also has a drying (astringent) effect on the tissues. The herb has a high tannin content, a chemical thought to help reduce skin inflammation. It may be prepared as a tea for the treatment of stomach problems and fever. Tormentil tincture is an alcoholic preparation of the rhizome and may be applied to small cuts to stem bleeding. An extract added to water may be used as a rinse or mouthwash to treat sore mouth and throat.

Family Rubiaceae Lady's Bedstraw
(Galium verum) Briwydden Felen

🌺 Small, narrow leaves that appear in whorls on the stems and bear numerous tiny, bright-yellow four-petalled flowers. Perennial. Height 15-60cm.
❀ Jun-Aug.

📍 Sand dunes. Also cliffs.

🍴 In the first stage of cheese making, the chopped flowering tops of the plant have the property to curdle milk. Rennet was used in the making of Cheshire cheese, its rich colour probably originally derived from this plant although the colouring is now obtained from annatto. It has been used in Gloucestershire for the same purpose, either alone or with the juice of the stinging-nettle.

📋 The leaves, stems and flowering tops may be used to treat kidney stones and urinary disorders in general, and as a tonic and diuretic. Also used as a poultice to treat skin infections, external ulcers and wounds.

✋ The name 'bedstraw' refers to its use as a stuffing for mattresses as it was reputed to repel fleas. The dried plant has the scent of newly-mown hay and was formerly scattered (strewn) over the floors of dwellings. Strewing herbs usually have fragrant or astringent odours and many also serve as an insecticide or disinfectant.

Family Saxifragaceae Rue-leaved Saxifrage
(Saxifraga tridactylites) Tormaen Tribys

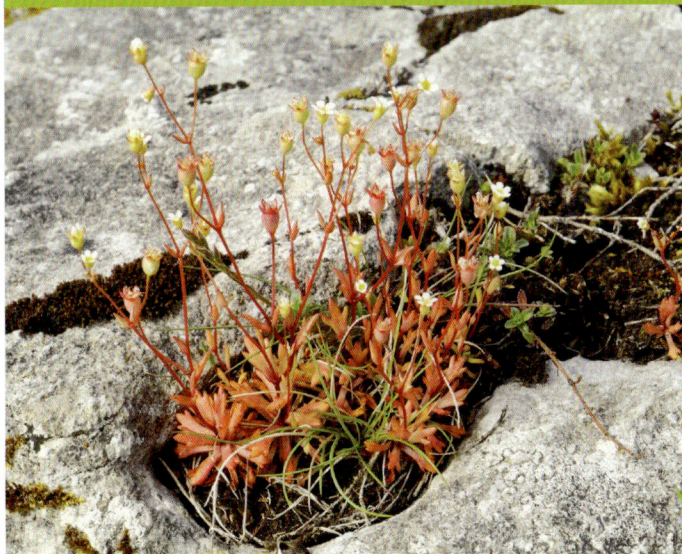

- Has distinctive, tri-lobed, fleshy leaves and red stems which are covered in numerous sticky glands. The erect flower stems bear small, white flowers. Annual. Height 10-50cm.
  - Mar-May.

- Dunes.

- As an annual, *S.tridactylites* is an exception as most plants in the genus are perennial.

Family Solanaceae   Duke of Argyll's Teaplant
(*Lycium barbarum*)

The long strap-shaped alternate leaves are greyish-green. Purple star-shaped flowers. The oval-shaped berries are bright orange-red. Deciduous woody perennial shrub.
Height 3m.
✿ May-Sep.

Sandy places near the sea. Shingle banks.

The fruit of *L. barbarum* (Goji berries) are very nutritious. They are high in fibre, protein and a range of vitamins and minerals including iron, copper, selenium and vitamins A and C. The berries may be eaten fresh or dried and added to foods such as muesli and yoghurt. A refreshing and healthy tea is also infused from the berries.

The fruit have been used as a traditional Chinese medicinal herb in Asian countries for more than 2000 years. Today the berries are considered a 'Superfruit' and health food as they contain high levels of vitamins, minerals and antioxidants. They are associated with many health benefits including protection against age-related eye diseases, promoting healthy skin, stabilising blood sugar, prevention of liver damage and as an aid to sleep. Animal studies have shown that Goji berry extract may help lower total cholesterol and triglyceride levels and increase 'good' HDL cholesterol.

Family Valerianaceae Common Cornsalad
(Valerianella locusta) Llysiau'r Oen

The tiny, pale lilac flowers are funnel shaped with 5 petals and occur in clusters. Large spoon-shaped, bright green leaves. Annual. Height 3-15cm. ❀ Apr– Jun.

Sand dunes. Also found on walls and waste ground.

The young leaves may be eaten raw and have a mild, nutty flavour and are suitable for addition to salads.

The leaves are rich in beta-carotene, an antioxidant which is converted into vitamin A in the body. This vitamin plays a role in iron metabolism, immune system health, growth, eyesight and skin health. It is also high in potassium, vitamin C and iron.

Family Veronicaceae   Heath Speedwell
(Veronica officinalis) Rhwyddlwyn Meddygol

The hairy green stems cover the ground in mats and send up vertical shoots which bear lilac-blue flowers. Perennial. Height to 40cm. ✳ May-Aug.

Heaths.

A pungent tea is made from the fresh flowering herb or the dried leaves.

The plant is no longer used in modern herbalism but the leaves and roots were once believed to be effective in the treatment of pectoral and nephritic complaints, haemorrhages, skin pro-lems and the treatment of wounds.

Family Violaceae Heath Dog-violet
(Viola canina) Fioled y Cŵn

Has long, oval pale green leaves and blue flowers with a narrow, straight spur. Perennial. Height 5-15cm. ❀ Apr-Jun. Near threatened.

Stable dunes. Also heaths and on various poor, acid soils.

The young leaves and flower buds may be eaten raw or cooked and used to thicken soups. A tea can be brewed from the leaves.

The flowers and leaves have powerful laxative properties and can also induce vomiting. Also used for treating skin problems.

Family Violaceae Dune Pansy
(Viola tricolour subsp. curtisii) Trilliw

The small flowers are yellow or pale blue and have 5 petals, the top two overlapping slightly. There are two smaller wing petals and a single large lower petal with radial reddish-brown honey guides. The leaves are toothed, oval with a heart shaped base. Annual. Height to 30cm.
Apr-Sep.

Sand dunes.

The leaves of wild pansies provide food for Fritillary Butterfly larvae.

Family Violaceae Common Dog-violet
(Viola riviniana) Gwiolydd Cyffredin

Flowers have 5 petals and are light blue with dark veins. Stout spur. The long-stalked leaves are heart shaped. Perennial. Height to 20cm. ✿ Mar-Jun.

Heaths and cliffs. Common elsewhere.

The young leaves and flower buds may be eaten raw or cooked and can be used to thicken soups. A tea may be brewed from the leaves.

FLOWERING PLANT INDEX OF PHOTOGRAPHS

FLOWERING PLANT INDEX OF PHOTOGRAPHS

GLOSSARY

Actinomorphic- a flower which is regular in shape and can be divided into two equal parts in any plane.

agg. - aggregate; a grouping of closely related species that are treated like as a single species for ease of identification.

Alternate - an arrangement where leaves grow singly at different levels on a stem.

Annual - a plant that completes its life cycle within one year.

Anther - the pollen sac carried at the tip of the filament. Anther and filament together constitute the stamen.

Antioxidant - a chemical that inhibits oxidation and removes potentially damaging oxidising agents in a living organism.

Astringent - a lotion applied to the skin to reduce bleeding from minor abrasions or as a cosmetic to counteract oily skin.

Axil - the angle between a leaf stalk and the stem from which it grows.

Basal - located at the base of the plant.

Biennial - a plant that germinates, grows leaves, stems and roots in the first year then enters a period of dormancy over the colder months. In the second year it will continue to grow, flower, produce seeds and die.

Bract - a leaf-like structure at the base of a flower stalk.

Calcareous - soils rich in calcium carbonate e.g. chalk, limestone or sea shells.

Calcicoles - plants that thrive on lime-rich soils.

Calcifuges - plants that cannot tolerate alkaline (basic) soils.

Decoction - a concentrated liquor resulting from heating or boiling a substance, especially a medicinal preparation made from a plant.

Demulcent - a gelatinous or oily substance that is capable of soothing inflamed or irritated mucous membranes and protecting them from further irritation.

Dioecious - a flower having male or female reproductive organs, not both.

Disc-floret - small, tubular flowers at the centre of the flower head of members of the daisy family.

Diuretic - a substance that increases the flow of urine.

GLOSSARY

Dune slack - a low-lying area within dune systems that are seasonally flooded and where nutrient levels are low.

Endangered - organism considered to be facing a very high risk of extinction in the wild.

Floret - a small flower, one of a group usually clustered together to form a flower head.

Genome - the complete set of genes or genetic material present in a cell or organism.

Halophyte - a salt-tolerant plant that grows in waters of high salinity, coming into contact with saline water through its roots or by salt spray.

Heath, heathland - a plant community on poor, acid soils.

Hemiparasite - a plant that obtains some nourishment from its host but is also capable of limited photosynthesis.

Humus- the organic component of soil, formed by the decomposition of leaves and other plant material by soil microorganisms.

Keel - two lower petals fused together at their bases that enclose the stamens and carpels.

Lanceolate - a leaf shaped like a lance head; tapering to a point at each end.

Leaflet - the separate leaf like structures of a compound or divided leaf.

Midrib - the central vein of a leaf.

Monoecious (hermaphrodite) - a flower having both male and female reproductive organs.

Near threatened - species which is close to qualifying for critically endangered, endangered or vulnerable.

Node - the point on a stem from which leaves, flowers or side shoots grow.

Opposite - (leaves) growing in pairs one on either side of the stem.

Ovary - female reproductive organ that contains the eggs or ovules.

Palmate - a leaf that is divided into leaflets which radiate from a single point of attachment i.e. shaped as in the palm and fingers of the hand.

Parasite - an organism that lives and feeds on or in an organism of a different species (the host) and causes it harm.

Perennial - a plant that grows for more than two years and may live for many years.

Petal - part of the inner ring of a flower; often brightly coloured but in some species may be absent.

Pinnate - a leaf that is divided into opposite pairs of leaflets.

GLOSSARY

Ray-floret - the outer strap-shaped florets in a compound flower of members of the daisy family.

Rhizome - a horizontal stem, usually growing underground and from which roots and growth buds emerge.

Rosette - a circular cluster of leaves arranged at or near the base of a stem.

Sepal - one of the outer rings of a flower, usually green, that encloses the petals in the bud.

Spike - a group of flowers all growing from a central stem.

Spur - in certain plants, part of a sepal or petal develops into an elongated hollow spike extending behind the flower, containing nectar.

Stamen -the male reproductive organ of a flower, consisting of a filament bearing an anther.

Strand line - a line, especially of washed-up seaweed or other debris, marking a previous high water level along a shore.

Succulent - having thick, fleshy, water-storing leaves or stems.

Tendril - extension of a leaf, usually coiling around other plants for support.

Transpiration - the loss of water by the plant by evaporation, chiefly from the minute pores or stomata on the leaves.

Umbel - a flower cluster in which stalks of nearly equal length spring from a common centre and form a flat or curved surface.

Vulnerable - facing a high risk of extinction in the wild.

Whorl - a group of three or more leaves or flowers growing in a ring from the same point on a stem.

Xerophyte - a plant adapted to live in a dry or physiologically dry habitat (salt marsh, saline soil or acid bog) by means of mechanisms to prevent water loss or to store available water.

Zygomorphic - (a flower) capable of being cut in only one plane so that the two halves are mirror images.

ACKNOWLEDGEMENTS

'Salt Marsh, Red Wharf Bay' (www.geograph.org.uk/photo/4428540)
© Copyright N Chadwick and licensed for reuse under creativecommons.org/licenses/by-sa/2.0

Flowering plant index of photographs

Photographs marked with asterisk * are by kind permission of Hugh Knott (www.cambriaflora.net)

Photographs without asterisk are from Shutterstock, except:

1 'Cochlearia danica (Danish Scurvy-grass) on cliffs near Crozon, France'
  (https://commons.wikimedia.org/wiki/File:Cochlearia_danica_Crozon_060416w.jpg)
  By User: Strobilomyces [GFDL (http://www.gnu.org/copyleft/fdl.html) or CC- BY-SA-3.0
  (http://creativecommons.org/licenses/by-sa/3.0/)], from Wikimedia Commons

2 'Inflorescence of Epipactis dunensis on Anglesey sand-dunes'
  (https://commons.wikimedia.org/wiki/File:Epipactis_dunensis_inflorescence.jpg)
  By Velella [CC BY-SA 3.0 (https://creativecommons.org/licenses/by-sa/3.0)], from Wikimedia
  Commons

3 'Limonium binervosum, Family: Plumbaginaceae, Image No. 3'
  (https://commons.wikimedia.org/wiki/File:Limonium_binervosum2.jpg)
  By Kurt Stüber [GFDL (http://www.gnu.org/copyleft/fdl.html) or CC-BY-SA-3.0
  (http://creativecommons.org/licenses/by-sa/3.0/)], via Wikimedia Commons

4 'Tephroseris integrifolia subsp. maritima on South Stack'
  (https://commons.wikimedia.org/wiki/File:Tephroseris_integrifolia_subsp.maritima.JPG)
  By Velella [CC BY-SA 4.0 (https://creativecommons.org/licenses/by-sa/4.0)], from Wikimedia
  Commons

ACKNOWLEDGEMENTS

5 'Tuberaria guttata subsp. breweri,' by Karen Woolley (https://karenwoolley.blogspot.co.uk)

6 'Arabidopsis thaliana'
(https://commons.wikimedia.org/wiki/File:Arabidopsis_thaliana.jpg)
Brona at en.wikipedia. User:Roepers at nl.wikipedia [GFDL (http://www.gnu.org/copyleft/fdl.html) or CC-BY-SA-3.0 (http://creativecommons.org/licenses/by-sa/3.0/)], from Wikimedia Commons

Other Titles by the author
Anglesey Flowering Plants and their Habitats   ISBN 978-1-5272-2578-7

Local organisations
For information on wildlife sites and nature reserves on Anglesey contact North Wales Wildlife Trust, Head Office, 'Llys Garth', Garth Road, Bangor, Gwynedd, LL57 2RT Phone: 01248 351541 Email: nwwt@wildlifetrustswales.org Website: www.northwaleswildlifetrust.org.uk
 For more information on Anglesey flora and if you are interested in botanical fieldwork and recording on Anglesey, contact the Anglesey Flora Group, c/o Treborth Botanic Garden, Bangor University, Treborth Road, Bangor, Gwynedd, LL57 2RQ Phone: 01248 353398
Email: treborth@bangor.ac.uk
The Botanical Society of Britain & Ireland (BSBI) is the centre for information on botanical matters throughout Britain and Ireland, with online up-to-date maps of the distribution of all species. Website: www.bsbi.org

NOTES

NOTES

NOTES